Henry Finch

REVERSING FALLS

ƧV

SurVision Books

First published in 2021 by
SurVision Books
Dublin, Ireland
Reggio di Calabria, Italy
www.survisionmagazine.com

Copyright © Henry Finch, 2021

Cover image: *Aubade Mountain* by Peter Richards
Copyright © Peter Richards, 2021

Design © SurVision Books, 2021

ISBN: 978-1-912963-22-5

This book is in copyright. No part of this publication may be reproduced, stored in a retrieval system, or transmitted in any form or by any means without the prior permission in writing from the publisher.

Acknowledgments

Grateful acknowledgment is made to the editors of the following, in which some of these poems, or versions of them, originally appeared:

05401 PLUS, About Place Journal, Crevice (Romania), Entropy, Forklift Ohio, GlitterMOB, jubilat, The Massachusetts Review, The Midwest Quarterly: A Journal of Contemporary Thought, The Missouri Review, North American Review, Prelude, and *Sugar House Review.*

"And Bright Snow" first appeared as "Kush," written for guitarist Ryan Blotnick's album *Kush* (Songlines Recordings, Canada).

Contents

Getaway Plans	5
Five Umbrellas	6
The Cheese-Eaters	7
Questions Passing Through Landscapes	8
Hoppin' John	10
When I Step on the Vegan Reuben	11
Guidelines for Survival	12
Blue Hill	13
Service Call	14
The Greatest Joy	15
Impressionism	16
Two for the Road	17
Always Together	18
Down by the Lake	20
Windsor	22
The Bear and the Hammer	23
Key Largo	24
Into Blossom	27
Morning Glories	28
Phase Music	29
A Kind of Reflex	30
Silk Scarf	32
Winding the Clock	33
And Bright Snow	34
Two Brothers	35
The Welcome Guest	36
This Is the Town	38

Getaway Plans

Speaking of galaxies,
what steady, deliberate pendulums you have,
what black eyes.
O mouthful of tennis ball,
I hereby request access to the President
as he/she greets a spotted doe.
You can drive a horse to burning oil
but you can't make him dance down the produce aisle,
and that's how diamonds are born.
Visions of lapdogs in matching grey sweatsuits.
Bulldoze the landfill into the sea,
howling along with the TV on your dashboard.
Generous creation of injury,
faces I've never been are disappearing.
Fire in a fitted linen suit,
here is a starburst worth of No.

Five Umbrellas

Into the telewardation
I hopelessly rummage xenopoodlewise,
reaparable as ever.
Underprotectionular I may be,
precracking
selfbutchered content
into anticoncretent of pseudoteardroptitude,
repairing the wheels of the disclandscaper,
recklessly throwing starlight
into the octomansplation, someone
I don't see myself becoming, someone's shadow
raises a rally of intraffictrophy,
seizing our abundant bouquets of probiefeasest
tied with the monolibertyhood of a yellow stripe.
I reach for both, leaning interarchwayly over
maximuseumesque expartnerless love,
instacarness kisses of macroPhiladelphiancy.

The Cheese-Eaters

We are all born of the same winter coats
the same jobs where bones meet
when all I want is the cinnamon Linda honestly
this tremor is all due to over-buttering in Massachusetts
serving you crossed-over caramel chains
useless roadside knotted flowers
a wilderness of earrings stranded at the airport
O but to embody the aroma of a cracked blue plastic seat
to lose yourself in a vehicle as kiwis roll across the windshield
across the sea a woman stretching what
her biscuit dough across a countertop
on Sunday morning Linda rings the bells
or presses play on a recording of the bells
to be projected over the main yard of the campus
as the dean is toasting you with artisan sourdough bread
until the cheese-eaters descend like crows into the Queso
Leonora a machine is sleeping humming idle
all its buttons wait for needless buttoning
teeth marks off the lips of Styrofoam cups
as moonlight smashes the evergreens
someone I become is drowning nearby
another paper bag is sinking
and I have to follow it into the night.

Questions Passing Through Landscapes

Are you now? Are you caught in a net?
Are you drifting downstream?
Are you part of a wave?
Are you the language of wind?
Are you a season? Are you July?
Are you the lace of a decade?
Are you emerging dappled by a canopy of ease?
Are you harmony between plucked strings?
Are you crossing the ocean on the back of a bee?
Are you glazed beside the river?
Are you tumbling through an old roof?
Are you a blanket of trust?
Are you a garden peppered with marigolds?
Are you the signal flashing in the valley?
Are you the cliff? Are you spreading your roots into sand?
Are you covering fruit with a sheet?
Are you leading me into the alpenglow?
Are you the dream of colors?
Are you home in the mouth of unknowing?
Are you a choir of fiddleheads?
Are you whitewater wearing down stones?
Are you propulsion? Are you a kingfisher nest?
Are you a village of steam?
Are you where sleep can find you?
Are you a foundation? Are you on a pier in the sound?
Are you outstretched for want of the truth?
Are you reflected? Are you the witness of morning?
Are you ushering fear through the wreckage?

Are you melting off a countertop?
Are you the probability of mutualism?
Are you finding a way through the dam?

Hoppin' John

Let beans soak for three days under
close supervision. Cook until evaporated.
Serve with a straw. Breathe
through a tube. Unfasten a few
buttons. Press the new mayor on
corruption. See below. Wash hands
immediately after use. Turn the tables
and take off in a dead run. Release the doves
over international waters. Write off
the floaters. Sink into a deep
depression. Open the steaming
buffet chafers and make yourself
at home. Shake yourself out
until there's nothing left. Hold an empty
press conference. Admit everything
to a room full of cardboard, hold yourself
over the fire, break like a wave, cry into
the minds of many, walk across
an open field and bury your
confession in the languorous shade.

When I Step on the Vegan Reuben

I take its rights
to a distant industrial landfill
and they cease to be.
Its center is soft
and its edges are toasted
inside a tall emerald fence.
The vegan Reuben crunches.
Its bones crumble and become dust,
dust that causes me to cough
in the landfill. "You may be yourself.
You may exist alone or in a symbiotic state.
You may be messy. You may be wicked,
but you may also meet me
at the airport," I say. Seitan is the first to go,
squeezing out between
rye bread. My boot reveals
a Russian dressing wound.
"You may not have this vegan Reuben," I say.
"I have stepped on it.
Just look at the sauerkraut,
like pickled slivered teeth.
Look how it smears so smoothly
when I drag the vegan Reuben across
the ground, how the caraway sounds like gravel."
"I didn't have this coming," it said.
"Life ought not to be cruel."

Guidelines for Survival

Say the wrong thing to the wrong
loaf of bread at lunchtime. Over-salt
a flesh wound. Leave your clothes downstairs
in the washing machine. Boil
the milk. Don't write back. Weed
out the annuals. Just up and slap
a dumpster door. Take your thumb
clean off gutting a fish in the yard
and let the boat run out of gas. Have to
flood the engine later. Kick the bucket. Fall
down the well. Throw the baby out with the
pharmacy umbrella. Get caught with a flimsy
coat in a downpour. Have too many drinks. Lose sight
of the entire afternoon. Let the good one get away.
Find God counting your breath but
lose your place and have to start over. Blow smoke
rings. Take up smoking. Take up jogging
every morning before work. Take up push-ups
before taking up swimming. Throw up
your hands. Ask for forgiveness. Waltz on
stage with the dance instructor. Make a habit
of buying schwag from someone named Trace.
Let a tooth rot right out of your mouth.
Overturn an upright piano two
weeks before your wedding. Learn to carve
a wooden duck in your neighbor's basement. Become wind
billowing sheets pinned to a clothesline.

Blue Hill

Unqualified blue cerulean shade blue bookish look blue don't be disappointed blue OK then be disappointed blue feeling blue curtains dissolve as you open them blue don't be discontented with the lack of February blue OK then be discontented blue be sad coffee blue this very blue pillow doesn't seem to mind blue blowing blue bubbles toward the blue heavens OK then toward the blue window blue coloring snow by way of miraculous bluestockings palming blue as blue backs bathe in the blue blissed backwaters Bluebeard bucketed barrels and basins through blue of blue polygamy in the blue room by the bayou blue libertines bundling bluebells in the blue blossoming spring the blueberry barrens in waiting bluebirds bundled in blue bushes as rain blows blue the rainbow too blue for this party blue blood in the lilies as beggars blow blue kisses to your nobility blue blowing the nobleman blue now bring me his blue-blooded face as Bacchus bows Boccherini blue on a backyard boulder blue intrinsic quilter of blue noble binding the Blue Book and baring your beautiful blue breasts in view of the bluecoats perfectly blue rounded blue devils blue fork tonguing the blue hallucination blues of bluefish suspended in ice I clawhammer bluegrass on the banjo blueing the atmosphere bluing affection imbuing hues of blue as I listen to the blue news a bluejacket smuggling blue jays into the hospital breaking blue joints under the blue light of Blue Monday OK then bleakly basking my buttered biscuits all Blue Monday long 'til the blue moon shoos my blue from room to room blue indefinite time of blueness I raise the Blue Peter I am leaving this teary-eyed port blue hoist the Blue Peter steer clear the blue buoy blue point us in the blue direction tie me to the blue mast with blue ribbon and fill my bluing billowing heart with blue ruin because the blues are not some blue thing you learn in blue uniform sauntering blue through town whistling a blue song surrounded by sadness as bluestockings urge blue pedants to take blue notice the blue affecters resonate blue chewing wadded blue stockings waking up bathed in a blue streak

Service Call

I answered the telephone. All I heard was gunfire
and shouting in a language I didn't understand,
crunching gravel, nearby and faraway
buildings blown to smithereens. Someone or something
shined a spotlight through the living room window
and cast my shadow onto the wall, but it was just a car
starting in the neighbor's driveway. "I have to go now.
Good luck with everything," I said, and hung up.
The horn blasted three or four times, headlights flashed,
the car pulled out of the driveway and vanished
down the dark street. My pulse was bounding
in my skull. A few dull embers glowed
in the fireplace and I stirred them with an iron poker.
The old house creaked in the wind. I thought it might
collapse. I called my brother. A groggy woman
answered. "Sirens and crumbling buildings,
wails of children, long whelps of dogs, grenades
exploding, glass shattering, shouts of pain and panic,
slow gears steadily churning and grinding
everything like coarse grains," I said.
"You're not making any sense. Good night," she said.
The poker trembled in my hand. I could not help
anything, and nothing could be helped.

The Greatest Joy

The reindeer stepped out of the box. Purple tinsel swayed from its antlers and a collar of sleigh bells jingled around its neck. "What language do you speak?" I said. The reindeer regarded me and smacked its tongue. "What do you miss the most?" it said. I did not want to seem ungrateful. I have witnessed brutal death in broad daylight, inconsolable shrieks of children in the throes of evacuation. There is love in my life, a head that rests against my breast, a waterfall we slip behind. "I miss to be near you," I said.

Impressionism

Hair of sea smoke as the evergreens cradle treetops
snapped loose after wind and freezing rain.
A nape of foxes
hunting house cats in the night.
Yours are the still eyes of the harbor
where ships rest and bounce against your lashes
anchored to the stones across the floor.
With a soul to house the hiding
below the laid planks of your tongue.
With hands that appear
like flickering candles in car windows. Your touch
as quiet as two exotic birds sleeping
in the backroom of the post office.
Yours is the voice of dew of blueberries
of lace painted with a palette knife.
Your breath of blooming irises
in an empty room. Silent as a sugar bowl
and crashing waves your heart
reveals and hides the sea
glass shards and lost oar locks.
Yours is the kiss of nesting swans.

Two for the Road

If I were you, I would be
lined with barbed wire,
tumbling onto the floor. The end.
Pencils down. Throw the kitten
off of the bridge. Don't take that road.
I need it. I'm guessing the wine is gone.
Beware the Cyclops and his sleeping
medication. You can't fly. Not yet,
at least. You're crazy for wanting to
fit that mattress up the stairs. She was
seeing somebody else. It wasn't just
the angel changing down in your bedroom
window that moved away. Now it's broken,
but that's OK. The power was shut off
in the middle of the dance party
anyway, so everyone staggered home
to mold in their basements.

Always Together

The product and the slim, constant decay.
The product and the wolf,
leaving the gallery together.
The product and the modern life,
listening to revolution songs
alone on headphones
at an airport gate. The product
and a handful of behind,
content with one half or the other.

The product and the reproductions
of this beautiful day
when nothing happens.
The product and the antler collection.

The product and the blame, rotating through the channels
on the satellite TV, staring at images

resulting from another flood.
The product and vacation weather,
more and more like a greeting card each day.
The product and what should be
and all the lines drawn onto the calendar.

The product with deceitful reason.
The product and the civilized,
eventually freezing with the elephants.
The product and no one.

The product and the streaming news, burning cities as the champagne bottles burst, throats cut fluidly unknown to the product.

Down by the Lake

"Why are you following me?" I said.
"I'm lonely," the devil said. He looked
at me from the corner of his eye.
Then he switched off the engine
and let out a long sigh.
His hairy red hands clutched the steering wheel.
"How about I buy us a couple of cold
sandwiches?" I said. "Sure," he said.
It looked uncomfortable for him to shift
his weight and pull himself out of the car,
and his horns kept getting caught
in the sagging roof lining. I bought our snacks
and joined him on the pier. We unwrapped
our sandwiches and took our first bites
in silence. I thought of the terrible people
he knew, the horror witnessed,
the inexpressible pain and immeasurable
suffering. "Thank you," he said.
We looked out together onto the choppy, black,
tumultuous water stirring with whitecaps.
"It's not your fault," I said. He picked off
a few crumbs and tossed them
in front of a duck. "Nothing's my fault.
I couldn't get a ticket if I crashed
a stolen ambulance into a church," he said.
His cloven hooves knocked on the pier
as he paced. A few onlookers
gathered and gawped. Soon protesters
would crowd with guitars and loudspeakers,
waving banners and poster board signs,

then an unruly mob armed with Molotov cocktails. "Things may not get better, but maybe they will, and that keeps me going." I said

Windsor

You dug up the grass
around the edge
and planted your bed
in my mouth.

I wanted you to lick my teeth,
but you thought I was joy.
You thought I was excitement
for the poppy in my crater.

I thought you might want
to scatter an ox
and watch it slowly grow
over my face.

You threw shovels.
You buried me
under a black Amy, a black Ingrid,
even a black Susan.

You sowed eight vines in morning.
You bedded your head in my chest.

The Bear and the Hammer

The bear was eating garbage on the steps of my apartment when I came home from the corner store. "You again," I said. "You look just like a bear when you're thinking," the bear said. But it was not a real bear. This was not even my home. "This is a dream. You are now a hammer," I said. And just like that the bear was a hammer, equipped with a worn red handle I immediately felt sorry for. What it must be like to be sledged about on top of nails, onto objects of disdain, and thrown carelessly into dark toolboxes. I raked my face and moaned loudly. I tore my shirt open. "What ecstasy! What a feeling to be alive and not be a hammer! I want to live and will not stand to not be held at night!" I said. The world grew saturated with pleasure, branches slowly drooped with the weight of luxuriant greens, heavy whipped clouds spilled across the neighbor's roof, and yet my own enraptured body stood unchanged. "This is not easy for me either," the hammer said.

Key Largo

There's a paradise behind Key Largo,
a beautiful, drunk Key Largo,
Key Largoing my golf cart for 350 dollars, fully addicted
to a Key Largo of the lost Atlantic,
borrowing a car and some Key Largo money,
rising from a youthful, geodesic Key Largo,
off-set and Key Largo as a used grenade,
a Key Largo sweating and sleeping, arched
over its own Key Largo, lapsing in and out
of Key Largo every day,
reduced to Key Largoing and yanking
from the foxy Key Largos,
kindred foxes that never Key Largo the door,
never wear their Key Largos inside
because they don't want to catch Key Largo,
Key Largoing from the outside.

The wrecking surf crashes Key Largo
over my feet as a descending dog Key Largos
onto the carpet, Key Largoing a hangover
from too much Key Largo, from that night
I filled the Crock Pot with Key Largos.

Everyone eventually learns to Key Largo a sailboat
because of their Key Largoism,
even though 9 in the morning is too early for Key Largo,
where everyone takes Key Largo in their water,
where the lantern lowlifes appear all of a sudden, Key Largoing
on and off, like Key Largos lighting up
the night sky, bright kernels of Key Largo,

taking ice in my Key Largo even though
we're all recovering Key Largos,
all after buying 100 Key Largos worth of groceries
and stepping outside for another quick Key Largo.

My family is made up of Key Largos, lapping lonesomely,
not capable of Key Largoing anyone, atrophied
from years of Key Largoing together,
even though 100 dollars of Key Largo is enough
Key Largo for me, enough for you to
just fucking love me, Key Largo,
even as Key Largos climb across the wall at night,
and if anyone wants a Key Largo,

then the shower drain will be clogged with Key Largos,
just as long as I keep my closest Key Largos
nearby, Key Largoing with exquisite knuckleheadedness,
wandering home to fire up the Key Largo,
hoping the constant Key Largo will keep
the mosquitoes away, acting like I never unKey Largoed
my luggage, even though I can Key Largo my laundry for free.

Surprises are made up of several smaller Key Largos,
like a roll of Key Largos on the handle of a plunger,
just before I tasted some kind of Key Largo in the water,
just before I learned I had to Key Largo the lid
before I flushed, otherwise flies would Key Largo,
before Key Largo was afraid
that someone would report my delinquent Key Largo
and discover the hull is filled with Key Largo and diesel fuel,
just because my Key Largo capsized,
just because everyone's skin is the color of Key Largo.
I'm trying to sell my Key Largo but I can't find the title,

looking for a release and that pair of dice behind Key Largo,
Key Largoing my associate's degree online and starting
to Key Largo on my bachelor's, not being able
to Key Largo at night because of the heat, and hurting, yielding
one step away from Key Largolessness,
elbowing my way though this Key Largorhea
and cracking open another cold can of Key Largo,
because it is the only way to fully Key Largo myself.

Into Blossom

I burst with my ear to your chest.
It is filled with splinters
and releases dust
as I lure the moths to my mouth.

The lilies shake champagne
onto the paws of a sleeping wolf,
but I decide when I am eaten.
I laugh and heads roll out of trees,
trees that tremble when I imagine them.

I step out of a crab and float through the rain
on an endless silk handkerchief.
I offer my voice, but it is locked in a cloud.
I open my jacket and feast upon the air.

And I blow out the sun.
And I am large.
As large as rain.
A bicycle passes through me.

Morning Glories

After the hydrant trumpets,
a lasso never goes by loop,
and a motorcycle is always.

May as well call blow the duck call
and take off with the burrowing spiders
as the red-faced porcupine
rustles in the strawberry beds.

A jackhammer rattles
out of a terrible nightmare
one-trip-let-and-trip into the lake.

Acrobats leapfrog in the sand.
I hear them all when I'm asleep.
O to be a dog in water.

Phase Music

and it just feels great to miss someone again
and it just feels great
to miss someone and adjust
feels great to miss someone
and adjust feels great
and adjust feels great to miss
great to miss to grate too
too great an attitude to grate
ingrates and grate two etudes to miss
to tomb to miss me too
to miss me miss missile
missed someone is someone
and someone is with someone
to summon one I'm one again on one
again on again and get on
and get someone get on and get it
and get it and get it someone get on
someone again and it's someone again
it's just again adjust and get in
adjust feels grey I just feed the grey eels
and it just ends it adjusts
just end it did ya end it
did ya dit dah dit dah dit dit dit dah
did ya adjust and adjust it just adjusts
and ya feel it again and again and again

A Kind of Reflex

There was a knock at the door. I didn't bother
asking who was there or looking through
the peephole. I didn't even announce myself
or hesitate with the knob in my hand.
A man was already talking and continued
after I opened the door. "If I can hide here,
if you can protect me, it would mean
the difference between several
and countless lives," he said.
He had not shaved in weeks, maybe longer,
and his shirt was threadbare. I could see
a blue kerchief through his breast pocket.
"I need to know a little more before I can
make that kind of decision. Would you
like a cold glass of water?" I said.
"Yes, that would be great. Everywhere
I go, people turn me away," he said.
"Where have you been?" I said.
"After the interrogations, I fled to the mountains,
towns so cold I couldn't find a tic come summer.
I'm so glad I found you," he said.
I passed him a glass of water
and he took a long drink
as he looked around the living room.
I didn't need to know any more
and sat down on the couch. "There's a piano
in the back room, an upright I inherited
from my grandmother. She played every day
until her fingers curled up with arthritis.
You can live behind it, in the coat closet.

We can make a pallet out of blankets," I said.
There were several knocks on the outside of the house,
then a brick crashed through the window.
"A day or two. Say I stole some food and fled," he said.
People were shouting outside, and I felt the walls
were closing in around us. "What is your name?
Who do you work for? Where are you going?" I said.
The man blew a whistle and the shouting stopped.
"Very impressive, Mr. Carol. We didn't know
if you had what is takes," he said.
"What it takes for what? My window is broken.
I thought you needed help," I said.
"The enemy will never suspect you," he said.
Then the man started laughing, and I started laughing,
but I didn't know why. He slapped my shoulder
and walked out the door. I never saw him again.

Silk Scarf

The silk scarf is whipped free
from an outdoor stand and wrapped
around the telephone pole split into two
under the force of sequential hurricanes which shred
the trailer park like tax forms perfectly julienned into piles
resembling iridescent tumbleweeds
tumbling across the landfill heat waves cause
to shimmer and smoulder in their vastness
through which the exiled trudge to return to a home
no longer their own occupied by whistling
birds on their perches while seismic shifts swallow
Volkswagen factories into the earth
like filo dough sculptures in a Kindergarten classroom
the message is brittle not long for this world
lucky to make it out of the building in an old shoebox
lined with cotton balls and glitter upon which is written
my love is an apple a river of apples.

Winding the Clock

Once upon a time, hidden in a dense, massive forest, there was a man who built and lived in a cabin for many years. He spoke to the trees and told jokes to roses and blackberry brambles. Every three days he wound the tall clock in one corner, turning the silver key into its fitting, listening to the gears tighten as a doctor does with a stethoscope over rising lungs. The bow of the key—the head of an owl, the hatch marks of its feathers worn smooth and tarnished— gave between his thumb and forefinger. His home fell into orbit, bumping celestial edges with faraway planets and moons. The owl's head broke off, and the shaft protruded from the clock face like a porcupine quill in the snow. He set the owl's head on the windowsill and took his cup of tea toward the door. He handled the knob, but it would not turn, so he shrugged. Through the kitchen window he watched a squirrel bathe in the seed of the bird-feeder. The knob would not turn, and when the man took it in the fabric of his shirttail, his hand only slid around the surface. He unlocked the window, slipped off his boots, and crowded his curled legs into the sink. The window would not budge, not as much as give a hint of giving way. And so the man sat in the sink and watched as the stranger emerged from the woods. He dragged a large leather sack that the other mistook for a serpent. He stood at the woodpile and surveyed the yard. A robin hopped in the grass, a shovel leaned against the well.

And Bright Snow

We pantomime in the illuminarium,
exchanging ours heads with pollen and grief.
We vamp against the candles making Copenhagen.

These are our regular hands, despite the need
for a seared grey currency. Ecstatic friction,
the lunar bird flutters through telephone octaves.
We mark the chords in her hair.

The stars are aloft, not weakening.
Reeds extend beyond their song as sleigh bells when given their distance,
a bright wet foal when she drawbridges.

Two Brothers

Once upon a time, in a place not worth naming, there lived two brothers. One brother was very rich and the other very poor. The rich brother had a beautiful wife, a son and a daughter, and a robust crop and vineyard that yielded a surplus of food and delicious wine of great renown. He wanted for nothing and spent his days enjoying the fruits of his labor. The poor brother's wife died giving birth to their first child, a daughter who moved far away. His garden turned to gravel and hardly yielded weeds, and he became known for stealing drinks from the bottoms of glasses. He wanted for nothing and spent his days mourning the withered fruits of his labor.

The Welcome Guest

I walked into a field on the edge of town. A crow watched from a treetop. A group of songbirds chattered in another. A jay swept between the clearing like a pendulum. This was the calm of my home. I shook some late leaves off a tree. A yellow flag waved above the castle on the mountainside. Grey clouds rippled as I passed along a trellis of roses and a man tending them with sheers. "Do you know who lives in the castle?" I said. The man turned around and studied the castle, which in the distance looked like a blurry grey mass. "I was born there," he said. "That's incredible. I've only seen the inside in photographs," I said. "Then you should go have closer look. Make yourself at home," he said. "Are you going to come with me?" I said. "No, I've seen it already, and besides, you'll never make it up the mountain," he said. "Why won't I make it?" I said. "Man-eating tigers, trip wires, and poison darts," he said. "I thought you wanted me to see your home," I said. "Insatiable leeches, briars like daggers, toxic mold spores. Do you believe in suffering?" he said. "Nothing I can't handle," I said. "And what about cowardice, foreclosure, and Sisyphean cycles of wealth?" he said. Two women passed us on a tandem bicycle. One woman pointed to us and the other snapped a photo with her camera. "Wolves waiting for you to rest, no sight of the stars, bees which burrow through bone," he said. "It must be beautiful," I said. "Thieves behind trees, quicksand, abject loneliness," he said. The yellow flag waved, and when I focused on it, it appeared to become larger. I felt I was nearing the castle already. "Broken glass, hypodermic needles, droves of rabid dogs," he said. "One foot in front of the other," I said. "Beds of hot coals, tedious bureaucratic procedures, cobwebs, tangles of razor wire," he said. "No one knows where I've been until I return and even then they never fully understand," I said. "Impenetrable fog, disembodied cries of fear," he said. The air stirred cold and the downpour was sudden. The clouds were confusing—charcoal smearing iridescence. Petals were ripped from the roses. The man gestured to the castle and spoke again, but his words were lost in the storm. Then he turned and began to walk toward the castle, receding into the landscape. Several buzzards circled over him and took turns diving at him. One buzzard dropped a writhing snake onto the man, then another flew off with his hat. A herd of wild boars emerged from the tall grass and chased after the man. He began to run and fell to the ground. A stampede of elephants tore across the field—each one ridden by a trumpeter who blew a chaotic banshee song into the rain. I watched the man disappear into the forest, followed by the bedlam. The flag flapped wildly. The same thing happens every day.

This Is the Town

You can thumb rides to a slim cigarette
in the shade. A boat knocks the pier
like a tired, floating metronome, clicking
its desperate, confusing,
last beats. Blue skies, black skies. Flat fields
of peanuts, tobacco, and smoke. The son picks
the grandmother off of the floor.
The mother takes take-out
and climbs into bed. A man drinks himself
right out of a tree. Another day falls from the roof.

I burned the recliner that broke yesterday,
a green effigy raked over the coals
and rustled to kick up some flames.
The embers glowed under the wire remains
and the lake lapped the shore as the radio played.
I fried up some fish, looked at the stars,
thought of the bills left unpaid,
then woke to the telephone ringing again.
Someone found a dog of mine an hour's drive away.

More poetry published by SurVision Books

Noelle Kocot. *Humanity*
(New Poetics: USA)
ISBN 978-1-9995903-0-7

Ciaran O'Driscoll. *The Speaking Trees*
(New Poetics: Ireland)
ISBN 978-1-9995903-1-4

Helen Ivory. *Maps of the Abandoned City*
(New Poetics: England)
ISBN 978-1-912963-04-1

Elin O'Hara Slavick. *Cameramouth*
(New Poetics: USA)
ISBN 978-1-9995903-4-5

John W. Sexton. *Inverted Night*
(New Poetics: Ireland)
ISBN 978-1-912963-05-8

Afric McGlinchey. *Invisible Insane*
(New Poetics: Ireland)
ISBN 978-1-9995903-3-8

Anatoly Kudryavitsky. *Stowaway*
(New Poetics: Ireland)
ISBN 978-1-9995903-2-1

Tim Murphy. *The Cacti Do Not Move*
(New Poetics: Ireland)
ISBN 978-1-912963-07-2

Tony Kitt. *The Magic Phlute*
(New Poetics: Ireland)
ISBN 978-1-912963-08-9

Clayre Benzadón. *Liminal Zenith*
(New Poetics: USA)
ISBN 978-1-912963-11-9

Thomas Townsley. *Tangent of Ardency*
(New Poetics: USA)
ISBN 978-1-912963-15-7

Matthew Geden. *Fruit*
(New Poetics: Ireland)
ISBN 978-1-912963-16-4

Marc Vincenz. *Einstein Fledermaus*
(New Poetics: USA)
ISBN 978-1-912963-20-1

George Kalamaras. *That Moment of Wept*
ISBN 978-1-9995903-7-6

Anton Yakovlev. *Chronos Dines Alone*
(Winner of James Tate Poetry Prize 2018)
ISBN 978-1-912963-01-0

Bob Lucky. *Conversation Starters in a Language No One Speaks*
(Winner of James Tate Poetry Prize 2018)
ISBN 978-1-912963-00-3

Christopher Prewitt. *Paradise Hammer*
(Winner of James Tate Poetry Prize 2018)
ISBN 978-1-9995903-9-0

Mikko Harvey & Jake Bauer. *Idaho Falls*
(Winner of James Tate Poetry Prize 2018)
ISBN 978-1-912963-02-7

Tony Bailie. *Mountain Under Heaven*
(Winner of James Tate Poetry Prize 2019)
ISBN 978-1-912963-09-6

Nicholas Alexander Hayes. *Amorphous Organics*
(Winner of James Tate Poetry Prize 2019)
ISBN 978-1-912963-10-2

John Bradley. *Spontaneous Mummification*
(Winner of James Tate Poetry Prize 2019)
ISBN 978-1-912963-13-3

John Thomas Allen. *Rolling in the Third Eye*
(Winner of James Tate Poetry Prize 2019)
ISBN 978-1-912963-15-7

Gary Glauber. *The Covalence of Equanimity*
(Winner of James Tate Poetry Prize 2019)
ISBN 978-1-912963-12-6

Charles Kell. *Pierre Mask*
(Winner of James Tate Poetry Prize 2019)
ISBN 978-1-912963-19-5

Alan Elyshevitz. *Mortal Hours*
(Winner of James Tate Poetry Prize 2020)
ISBN 978-1-912963-21-8

Maria Grazia Calandrone. *Fossils*
Translated from Italian
(New Poetics: Italy)
ISBN 978-1-9995903-6-9

Sergey Biryukov. *Transformations*
Translated from Russian
(New Poetics: Russia)
ISBN 978-1-9995903-5-2

Alexander Korotko. *Irrazionalismo*
Translated from Russian
(New Poetics: Ukraine)
ISBN 978-1-912963-06-5

Anton G. Leitner. *Selected Poems 1981–2015*
Translated from German
ISBN 978-1-9995903-8-3

message-door: An Anthology of Contemporary Surrealist Poetry from Russia (bilingual)
Edited and translated from Russian by Anatoly Kudryavitsky
ISBN 978-1-912963-17-1

Seeds of Gravity: An Anthology of Contemporary Surrealist Poetry from Ireland
Edited by Anatoly Kudryavitsky
ISBN 978-1-912963-18-8

All our books are available to order via
http://survisionmagazine.com/books.htm